# WALKING WITH
# ROMANS

## BECOMING THE MAN GOD INTENDS YOU TO BE

Carriage
House
PUBLISHERS

## A 30-DAY DEVOTIONAL
## AND BIBLE STUDY

### FRED J. PARRY

# WALKING WITH ROMANS

**Published by**
Carriage House Publishers
Library of Congress Control Number: 2022902468
Paperback ISBN: 979-8-9857824-0-0
eBook ISBN:978-1-0879-2643-8
Cover Design by Debbie Lewis
Interior Design by Carolyn Preul
Copy Editing: Melody Parry
Theological Review: Patrick K. Miller
Printed in the United States of America

## ACKNOWLEDGMENT:

Special thanks to my friend Patrick Miller for his expert and unabashed guidance during the writing and editing of *Walking With Romans*. Patrick graduated from Covenant Theological Seminary and oversees digital ministries at The Crossing in Columbia, Missouri. He has written for *The Gospel Coalition* and *Christianity Today* and is the co-author of the forthcoming book *Truth Over Tribe*. Patrick offers cultural commentary on the podcast *Truth Over Tribe* and teaches on *Ten Minute Bible Talks*. He is married to Emily, and they have two kids.

For my wife, Melody, who has endured a courageously fought battle with cancer over these past four years. By God's grace and healing powers, she has demonstrated how victory is won through her steadfast faith in Jesus. She is an inspiration not only to me and our two sons but to everyone who has witnessed her journey through this chapter of her life. May every man who reads this be blessed by such a woman.

………

*"God is in the midst of her;*
*she shall not be moved; God will help*
*her when morning dawns."*

**(Psalm 46:5)**

# CONTENTS

For more information on using this book for a group study,
please visit **www.FredParry.Life** for study materials,
handouts, and other useful information.

# INTRODUCTION

## A REASON FOR HOPE

*"For I am not ashamed of the gospel, because it is the power of God that brings salvation to everyone who believes: first to the Jew, then to the Gentile."*
*(Romans 1:16 NIV)*

In 57 AD, just three decades after Jesus' death and resurrection, the Apostle Paul was preparing for a missionary journey to modern-day Spain. He hoped to stop over in Rome to raise financial assistance for his trip, but he had two significant challenges he would first have to overcome.

Because Paul did not plant the church in Rome, he did not know many people there. Unlike with the churches he planted in Ephesus, Corinth, and other cities, Paul would have to build trust and establish a relationship with the members of the Roman church.

At this time, the church in Rome was suffering from great internal division. Both the Gentiles and the Jews who had become Christian converts wanted to worship in separate communities. A divided church was not only problematic for Paul's missionary purposes, but the internal strife would also make it more difficult to represent Jesus to the Roman Empire's most cosmopolitan and influential city.

In many ways, the dynamics Paul faced in Rome are not unlike what we face today. As with Paul, the divisions we are currently experiencing seem insurmountable. We live in a divided society rife with conflict. There is extreme polarity in the political, cultural, and theological realms of our lives. The idea of reaching consensus, compromise, or just a basic level of tolerance for those with different beliefs seems all but impossible. Within our own society, there are deep divides in opinion about social equity, race relations, and even gender identity. We seem to have reached an impenetrable impasse.

At the time of the writing of this devotional, the world has suffered through nearly two years of the COVID-19 pandemic. This global health crisis has essentially put a gigantic magnifying glass on the lack of trust and civility that exists in our present culture. Emotions are high. Tensions have flared. Politicians wax poetically about the "good old days" when a terrorist attack on the United States brought together our then-divided country. These are desperate times, indeed.

I believe that hope can be found in Paul's writings to the church in Rome. Once our differences are put into their proper context and approached with a sense of love and humility, the matters that currently divide us are minuscule in comparison to the matters that can unite us. Paul reminds us of the promise made to us by God has the divine power to bring us all together.

As Christians, we have a responsibility to represent Jesus in our communities. What would Jesus do in light of the current conflict we are experiencing? The book of Romans offers a refreshing insight and perspective on how we can initiate the change and reconciliation that needs to take place. The playbook has been written. The solutions to our problems were prescribed by Christ and then recorded by Paul some 2,000 years ago.

Our sin is what has always kept us from God, blocking us from the joy and contentment that so often seems evasive. Unfortunately, we allow this sin to control us rather than making room for the Holy Spirit in our lives. Through his letter to the Roman church, Paul beautifully weaves the wisdom from the Old Testament with the sacrifice of Christ to show us that there is a better way. From the faithfulness of Abraham to the passivity of Adam, we have examples of how we can get our lives, and the rest of society, back on the right path.

As Paul mentions in Romans 1:16, he is not ashamed of the gospel. The same should be true for us because God's word offers the peace and hope needed to navigate these trying times. Keeping this good news to ourselves would be selfish and cruel.

I hope you enjoy this study of the book of Romans. My prayer is that it will bring you the comfort, confidence, and satisfaction of knowing that the answers to life's challenges and problems can be found through our relationship with God. Nothing can separate us from our loving Father and that should be the source of everlasting joy and hope.

Fred J. Parry

# OVERVIEW OF PAUL'S EPISTLE TO THE ROMANS

The Epistle to Romans was written around 57 A.D., while Paul was in Corinth near the end of his third missionary trip, more than three decades after the death and resurrection of Christ. It is believed that Paul likely dictated this letter to a disciple named Tertius, who served as his assistant. The letter was then personally delivered to the Roman church by Phoebe, a well-respected deacon and generous benefactor for Christians in the church at Cenchreae, near Corinth.

The book of Romans, as it is also known, is the longest of the Pauline Epistles. It is the sixth book in the New Testament but is placed first among Paul's 13 letters implying a special significance of the letter, likely due to its thorough explanation of core Christian ideas, or what theologians call "doctrine." It is said to be the most theologically significant and the most comprehensive explanation of the gospel that tells the story of Jesus' life, death, and resurrection.

The version of Romans we know today is 16 chapters long, but over the centuries, it has been published in 14 and 15 chapter versions. Biblical scholars describe Paul's letter to the Romans as "overwhelming" and a "work of massive substance." Nearly all of the core doctrines of Christianity can be found in this one letter.

## PAUL'S MESSAGE TO ROMANS

Paul's letter to the Roman church presents several key teachings that are integral to understanding Christian doctrine. Major themes in the letter include the concepts of righteousness, justification, sanctification, and glorification. Throughout the letter, Paul correlates several Old Testament references to illustrate that Christ was indeed the Messiah (a Jewish title given to kings) and that God had kept his promise to the nation of Israel. Paul also used the letter to drive home the controversial message that both Jews and Gentiles would have equal access to the salvation granted to believers.

Paul employs the frequent use of questions through this letter to move his arguments forward. Interestingly enough, Paul poses no fewer than 85 questions in his letter to Romans to challenge his readers and to get them thinking about the concepts he is presenting. Paul often wrote in a style known as a diatribe, in which he anticipated and answered the challenges and objections he expected to draw while presenting important aspects of church doctrine. For that reason, the style of his writing, at times, may come across as argumentative or defensive.

## ANCIENT ROMAN

At the time of the writing of this letter, Rome was the capital of the Roman Empire and the epicenter of cultural and political activity. Biblical scholars believe that between three and four million people were living in Rome at that time.

Paul, however, was not the founder of the Roman church. It is believed that the church there was founded by Jews who had been on a pilgrimage to Jerusalem and became Christians on the Day of Pentecost (Acts 2). Another theory suggests the church was started by Christians who had migrated from churches planted by Paul in Asia, Greece, and Macedonia. While these Jews believed in Christ, they still held on to tenets of Mosaic law as prescribed in the Torah.

Around A.D. 54, the church in Rome suffered a tremendous setback when the Roman Emperor Claudius expelled all Jews from Rome because of the frequent public disturbances that would erupt as a result of the disagreements between Christian Jews and non-Christian Jews. After five years had passed, Jews were allowed to return to Rome by Claudius's successor, Nero, but by that time, their church had become divided and Gentile Christians had taken control of the church. Christian Jews felt marginalized and excluded from church leadership. There was great tension between those who were considered "weak in faith" and those who considered themselves "strong in faith." Paul's goal was to restore unity to the Roman church so that he to endure its westward expansion.

At the time Paul wrote this letter, he had never visited Rome; however, he seemed to have a familiarity with at least 25 members of the church as he refers to them by name in Romans 16. Paul also specifically references one of the house churches he was aware of that was meeting in Rome. Many

Romans were somewhat skeptical about Paul's visit because he was regarded as a controversial figure. Because of this, Paul's letter was written to serve multiple purposes. On one hand, it was Paul's way of preparing the Romans for his visit and to make clear the purpose of his stop en route to Spain. He used the letter to communicate a rather in-depth explanation of Christian doctrine to show that he was well-versed and respectful of both Old Testament teachings and Mosaic law. Paul also hoped the letter would help him raise funds to support his mission to Spain.

Paul was planning to travel to Rome after a stop in Jerusalem. Paul had some trepidation about returning to Jerusalem because he had been warned about potential hostilities and possible imprisonment awaiting him. However, he provided ahead despite the warnings. Once arriving in Jerusalem, he was arrested and imprisoned in Caesarea for two years (Acts 23-25).

Paul eventually made it to Rome, but went there to appear before Caesar on the charges brought against him in Jerusalem (Acts 28). Once in Rome, he stayed under house arrest for more than two years where he was allowed to continue to teach and spread the message of Christianity.

## MAJOR THEMES

The 16 chapters of the Epistle to Romans can be broken down into four separate themes:

- **Chapters 1-4** reveal God's righteousness. God saves those who believe in the sacrificial death and resurrection of Jesus. It is stressed that God fulfilled the promises made to Abram and Jacob in Genesis 12:1-20. Paul makes it clear that humanity is plagued by the destructive power of sin and that the Jews are just as guilty of these sins as the Gentiles. Paul reminds his readers that Jesus took away our sins in the fulfillment of God's promise. Jesus became what we are so that we might become who he is. Paul makes it clear that we have been justified by faith and not by our deeds. We have a new status before God. Jews and Gentiles are both now part of God's family with a bright and promising future.

• **Chapters 5-8** outline the creation of a new humanity climaxing in the renewal of all creation and Paul makes his best case to assure his readers of their salvation through Christ. Paul shows that we are joined with Jesus through our faith and calls us to set aside our old ways and surrender to the will of God.

• **Chapters 9-11** again show how God has fulfilled the promises he made to Israel. Paul emphasizes that God included Gentiles into Abraham's family with the hope that Israelites would grow jealous, set aside their unbelief, and return to him. We are invited into God's family and are drawn to him as we learn of the creation, the fall, the redemption, and the restoration of God's kingdom.

• **Chapters 12-16** outline Paul's attempts to unify the Roman church. By emphasizing that the gospel can lead to a transformation and the "renewing of one's mind," Paul establishes how Christians should live once they have been saved by the grace of God and no longer bound by the law of Moses. Paul reminds us to set aside our own ambition and to serve others sacrificially. Paul finally calls his readers to live in fellowship with one another.

To gain a better understanding of the context surrounding Paul's letter to the Romans, spend time reading the Book of Acts. You'll find that 16 of the 28 chapters in the Book of Acts focus on Paul's life and works as a disciple.

# THE APOSTLE PAUL

P aul was born in the city of Tarsus, a major city in eastern Cilicia on the trade route between Syria and Asia Minor, which was located in the same geographical region as modern-day Turkey. Born the son of a Pharisee and in the ancestral lineage of the Tribe of Benjamin, Paul enjoyed the unique distinction of being a Jew and the privilege of being a Roman citizen. He could speak Hebrew but his native tongue was Koine Greek. Paul was educated at the prestigious Rabbinical school taught by Gamaliel, who is thought to be one of the most influential rabbis in the history of ancient Judaism.

Next to Jesus, Paul is considered the second most important figure in the history and growth of Christianity. He is believed to be the author of 13 of the 27 books in the New Testament. While there is some scholarly debate as to the complete authenticity of some books in the New Testament, experts acknowledge that at least seven of the 13 letters from Paul are undisputed as authentic works. Romans is an undisputed letter.

## PAUL'S CONVERSION

Readers of the New Testament first encounter Paul as "Saul of Tarsus." Although Saul was a tentmaker by trade, he was also a fervent persecutor of early Christians. In Acts 9:1-22, we read of Saul traveling from Jerusalem to Damascus during his crusade

# TRAVELS OF THE APOSTLE PAUL

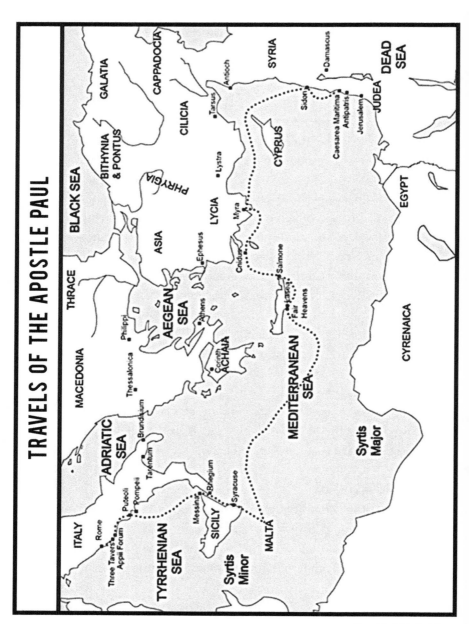

to arrest disciples when he encounters the resurrected Jesus in a great light. During this experience, Jesus reveals to Saul that he is Lord and that persecuting his followers is the same as persecuting the Lord Jesus and is, in effect, fighting against God. N.T. Wright conjectures that during this journey, Paul was repeating a prayer, used by many serious Jews in his day, requesting a visionary experience of God. An answer to that prayer was surprising enough, but seeing Jesus in the place of Yahweh literally reconfigured Paul's worldview.

During this encounter, Saul was temporarily blinded by the light that surrounded the vision of Jesus. In spite of this, he traveled on to Damascus where he remained blind for three days. Saul took no food or water for this period and stayed in a constant state of prayer until approached by a disciple named Ananias. Ananias told Saul that he had been sent by Jesus to restore his sight and assured Saul that the Lord would fill him with the Holy Spirit. Once Saul's sight was restored, he was immediately baptized and became a fervent believer in Jesus Christ.

## MISSIONARY TRIPS

Following his baptism, Paul went on to Arabia and Damascus and began to preach that Jesus was indeed the Messiah. It was soon thereafter that he, himself, began to be persecuted for his teachings. Around A.D. 37, nearly three years after his conversion, Paul traveled to Jerusalem where he met for 15 days with James, the half-brother of Jesus, and the Apostle Peter. Paul used these meetings to learn more about the life of Jesus and to report on his efforts in preaching about the Kingdom of God and Jesus the Messiah. Over time, Paul became known as the

"Apostle to the Gentiles," while Peter was known as the "Apostle to the Jews."

Soon after Paul met with James and Peter, he returned to his hometown of Tarsus to preach until he was invited by Barnabas to go and teach at the rapidly growing church in Antioch. It was there where Paul began to build a network of house churches at which the earliest Christians would gather at the homes of other followers until the size of the group forced them to divide into smaller groups. Antioch was also the first place where Jewish-Gentile churches took root. This is why, in Acts 15, Paul and Barnabas go to meet with the apostles and discuss whether Gentile converts needed to be circumcised. With limited resources, Paul and Barnabas often relied on the generosity of their converts for food and housing. In A.D. 47, Paul returned to Jerusalem with Barnabas and brought famine relief contributed by the early churches they had started. In this respect, Paul was, perhaps, the earliest pioneer of missionary work that would be done by churches in the coming centuries.

Paul and Barnabas then set out from Antioch on the first of three mission trips where they visited Cyprus and Galatia. Hoping to build unity between Jews and Gentiles for the benefit of God's kingdom, Paul attended the Council of Jerusalem in A.D. 49 to successfully argue that Gentiles should not be required to follow Jewish Law in order to become Christians. It is around this time in scripture where Saul begins being referenced as Paul. Historians speculate that Paul was actually Saul's Roman name and that the names may have been used interchangeably for some time so that he could more easily relate to a diverse variety of audiences.

On his second missionary trip, Paul traveled with Silas through Asia Minor and Greece and settled in Corinth, where he stayed for three years. It is believed he wrote his letters to the Thessalonians there. After short stints in Jerusalem and Antioch, Paul began his third missionary trip and settled in Ephesus.

In Ephesus, Paul wrote his epistles to the Galatians and Corinthians. He stayed in Ephesus for three years and built strong relationships using this central location along heavily traveled trade routes to spread Christianity through a vast region. Armed with the Holy Spirit and his ability to converse with both Jews and Gentiles, Paul went on to plant several churches throughout the Asia Minor, Greece, and Macedonia. Along the way, the Lord performed several miracles through Paul including healing a crippled man at Lystra (Acts 14:8-18), raising Eutychus from the dead in Troas (Acts 20:8-12), and healing a woman who had been possessed by an evil spirit (Acts 16:18).

## THE CAPTIVITY EPISTLES

Throughout his ministry life, Paul was jailed on numerous occasions and placed under house arrest for extended periods. It was during these periods that Paul crafted several of his letters to the churches he had planted. Because these letters were written while he was imprisoned, they are often referred to as the "Captivity Epistles."

In Acts 16:16-34, we read that Paul and Silas were imprisoned in Philippi for disturbing the peace after casting a demon out of a slave girl. While imprisoned, a sudden earthquake brought down the walls of the jail. Paul and Silas made the conscious decision not to escape, and this led to what would become a trusted relationship with their jailer, who would later become a follower of Christ. In A.D. 57, Paul returned to Jerusalem and was soon arrested and jailed for taking a Gentile too far into the precincts of the temple. These were false accusations, based on faulty assumptions, but they caused enough upheaval to gain Roman attention (Acts 22:29).

During his captivity in Jerusalem, Paul defended his actions before the Sanhedrin. His testimony divided the Sadducees and Pharisees who had strong disagreements over whether Paul had broken any laws. Roman authorities then took Paul, with an armed escort to Caesarea for higher officials to to hear the case. Paul remained there for several years, and despite his innocence, was not released. Biblical tradition reports that a Roman official was trying to extort a bribe from him (Acts 24:26). Finally, exasperated, Paul asked to make his appeal to Caesar himself.. After his request was reluctantly granted, Paul was placed on a ship, as a prisoner, to sail to Rome. On that voyage, he was shipwrecked on the island of Malta for three months where he performed miracles and continued to preach the word of God.

When Paul finally arrived in Rome, he was placed under house arrest but was allowed to continue preaching without interruption from authorities. During this time, Paul wrote his letters to the Philippians, Ephesians, Colossians, and Philemon. Upon his release, it is believed that Paul then traveled to Spain where he wrote his letters to Timothy and Titus.

## PAUL'S DEATH SENTENCE
In A.D. 64, Paul returned to Rome where he was martyred. While

little has been written regarding the details surrounding Paul's death, tradition has it that Paul was sentenced to death by the Roman Emperor Nero. Paul's death sentence came shortly after a large portion of Rome, filled mostly with tenements for the poor, burned in a fire. Nero blamed the fire on Christians, though Roman documents suggest that Nero started the fire himself to clear space for a building project. Because Paul was a Roman citizen, he was exempt from death by crucifixion. Instead, he was decapitated by a sword. In the end, Paul died because of his faith. In his final writings, it was clear that Paul was ready and willing to die for Christ; giving his last breath for the cause of helping the first generation of Christians understand that sacrifice was an essential part of following Christ.

FJP

# HOW TO USE THIS BOOK

**W**alking with Romans: Become The Man God Intends You To Be is designed to serve the dual purpose of being both a daily devotional and a Bible study guide for the New Testament's Book of Romans. While the book is structured to be used over a six-week period, I would encourage you to use it at a pace that is most comfortable for you.

Each of the daily devotions is inspired by a passage in Paul's letter to the Roman church. From these passages, I have found themes that can guide us in our daily walk to become better Christians. From these 16 chapters, you will discover important teachings from Paul on God's righteousness, the new creation, the destructive power of sin, and gain some insight into how Old Testament prophecy is played out as promised by the death and resurrection of Christ. These devotionals were written as responses from my own personal understanding of how a particular passage spoke to me. The goal of any Bible Study is to find the correct interpretation which leads to a variety of applications. That, in itself, is rightly handling the word of truth (2 Timothy 2:15).

If you're like me, you'll get a new insight or meaning each time you read one of these passages and not because the Bible's meaning has changed, but because we, as individuals, have changed since the last time we were there. We've become more aware of a different aspect of our lives, and this Scripture now speaks to us in a new way. We are more teachable than we were before. The Bible takes us on where we are, and God uses His Word to lead us to greater maturity and a broader perspective. The Bible is as deep as we are and deeper still.

I would suggest approaching each devotional in prayer, asking God for clarity of mind and focus with a hope that the day's message resonates with you in some meaningful way.

Once you've read the devotional, you'll find the following tools at the end of each reading to help you get the most meaning out of the day's message:

- A reference to scripture outside the Book of Romans that will reinforce and add context to the day's message;

- Next, you'll find two short questions designed to help you apply that day's lesson to your life;

- Finally, you'll find a call to contemplate which is intended as a prompt for journaling. It's an excellent opportunity to explore and record your feelings as they relate to the day's message.

To gain a better understanding of the literary and cultural context of each day's passage, I would encourage you to refer to the full text each day to fully understand the contextual circumstances and events surrounding each passage. Most of the passages quoted come from the New International Version (NIV) of the Holy Bible.

I hope that you'll find these devotionals to be useful and relevant in your daily walk. My prayer is that the wisdom that comes from Paul's letter to the Romans will guide you in your journey to lead a more fulfilling and Christ-centered life.

FJP

# 15 RULES OF ENGAGEMENT FOR SMALL-GROUP STUDIES

1. Nothing said in the group gets discussed outside the group!
2. Be transparent. Be authentic. Be your true self.
3. Everyone needs to share, both as a speaker and a listener.
4. Encourage one another. Speak truth into each others' lives while avoiding the temptation to "fix" another person in your group.
5. Challenge each other. It's reasonable to disagree, but always respect boundaries.
6. Give your darkest issues the light of day. You'll find that sharing your sin can be incredibly liberating!
7. Be willing to be vulnerable. Take a chance to let your risk be rewarded.
8. We all have blind spots. Dare to explore what yours might be.
9. Absolutely NO gossip. Nothing erodes trust faster than gossip.
10. Embrace your mistakes. Take ownership of your weaknesses, knowing that we're all human.
11. Resist the urge to rescue others when they struggle to find the right words. Let people finish their thoughts at their own pace.
12. Don't be afraid of silence. Pause and feel the weight of what has been shared.
13. Trust is our most important currency. Earn it and then be willing to extend trust to others.
14. Side conversations are a sign of disrespect; only one voice at a time.
15. When possible, find time to connect with each other outside the small group setting.

*"For all have sinned and
fall short of the glory of God,"*

**(Romans 3:23 NIV)**

# WEEK 1

# BOLD IN FAITH

*"For I am not ashamed of the gospel, because it is the power of God that brings salvation to everyone who believes: first to the Jew, then to the Gentile. For in the gospel the righteousness of God is revealed—a righteousness that is by faith from first to last, just as it is written: "The righteous will live by faith." (Romans 1:16-17 NIV)*

Depending on your personal circumstances, it might be difficult for you to boldly proclaim the good news of Christ. Perhaps you live in a liberal college town like I do where self-proclaimed "enlightened" individuals among us tend to roll their eyes or give a dismissive look when the subject of God comes up. Maybe you struggle with consistency in trying to live out a Christian life and you don't want to be called a hypocrite when you slip up from time to time. Whatever the reason, Paul calls us to set aside our shame and recognize the good news of Christ for its ultimate purpose...to save the lives of the people we love. As we grow in our spiritual maturity, Paul encourages us to push through the awkwardness and discomfort we may feel and trust God's plan.

The gospel is for everyone, not just a chosen few but also those who may not necessarily deserve to hear the good news. Because of God's promise to Abraham for his descendants, it was important for Jews to hear the message of salvation first. Logically, this made sense because the Jewish citizens of Rome had the best understanding of the God of the Old Testament. When they failed to recognize that Jesus was the Messiah that God had promised to send, Paul turned to the Gentiles knowing they would play a major role in growing God's church.

There are, after all, strong similarities between Judaism and Christianity and we must focus on the abiding truth that in which unites us is far greater than anything that divides us. Christians believe in the Holy Trinity where God is three in one; God the Father, God the Son, and God the Holy Spirit. In Judaism, followers cling to the belief that God is one and indivisible. Jews dispute the notion that God could have a son and send him to the earthly world.

In the end, the gospel we share as Christians doesn't force unbelievers to take one side or the other. The gospel we share is God's dynamic and powerful way of giving his beloved children the gift of unending life with him in a renewed creation. Sharing the good news of God's kingdom is an important mark of what it means to live a good and fulfilling Christian life. Some would argue convincingly that if you personally believe that rejecting Jesus leads to destruction, it is an act of profound selfishness not to share him.

## MY PRAYER
*God, help me to be bold in my faith. Wipe away my shame and insecurities so that I can share the good news of the salvation you've promised to those who follow you. I pray for these things in the name of your son, Jesus Christ. Amen.*

## READ: 1 CORINTHIANS 16:13

**QUESTION #1:** What are the obstacles that prevent you from sharing the good news of the gospel?

**QUESTION #2:** What person among your circle of friends or family members do you believe would be the most difficult to share with the Gospel?

## CONTEMPLATE

Make a list of the people in your life who would benefit from hearing about the good news of God. What details from your personal journey would you be willing to share?

# THE ULTIMATE JUDGE

*"You, therefore, have no excuse, you who pass judgment on someone else, for at whatever point you judge another, you are condemning yourself, because you who pass judgment do the same things. Now we know that God's judgment against those who do such things is based on truth. So when you, a mere human being, pass judgment on them and yet do the same things, do you think you will escape God's judgment? (Romans 2:1-3 NIV)*

One of the most important things I did in the early stages of my Christian journey was to join a small group of men who vowed to hold me accountable. I gave these men permission to ask me the tough questions and call me out when they sensed I was lacking an appropriate level of authenticity. Thanks to this group's pledge to be transparent with one another, the more they knew about my sin, the harder it was for me to hide. Every man in this group was held to the same standard. As much as we knew about each others' struggles, temptations, and brokenness, we often found ourselves judging other men outside of our small group. As hard as we tried, we couldn't resist the temptation to be the judge, jury, and executioner regarding the failings of others.

Looking back, I now know that my actions disappointed God. Paul teaches us that God is the only righteous judge. The sin we see most often in others probably has much more to with our own sin versus that of the person being judged. When we condemn others, we're actually doing greater harm to our standing before God because we make it obvious that we have become blind to our own sin. Jesus told a story about a man whose master forgave an unpayable debt. Later on, that same man threw a friend in debtor's prison for a tiny debt. When his master heard what was done, he was livid. How often do you do the same thing? Jesus forgave a lifetime of your sin, but you're ready to lay the hammer on anyone who wrongs you in the slightest way (Matthew: 18:21-35).

Worse yet, somewhere along the way, we made up our own rules of the game when we decided that certain types of sin were socially acceptable and not worthy of God's wrath or attention. In Matthew 7:1, we are instructed, "Do not judge, or you too will be judged. For in the same way you judge others, you will be judged, and with the measure you use, it will be measured to you." For reasons unknown, we tend to live by the lie that our sins don't compare to the sins of others. To be clear, God doesn't care what we think of sin. In God's courtroom, there's no room for subjectivity, inconsistency, or misrepresentation of the facts. God's judgment is absolute and final. The next time you feel the urge to judge another man's actions, run for the nearest mirror and take a good, hard look at yourself.

## MY PRAYER
*God, in your infinite wisdom, you are the only judge that matters. Focus my eyes on my own failures and sinfulness and guide me to walk straight in the pursuit of the righteousness I may never achieve. May I walk in humility for the remaining days of my life. Amen.*

## READ: MATTHEW 7:1-6

**QUESTION #1:** Which of your sins do you believe is the least offensive to God?

**QUESTION #2:** Recall a time when you incorrectly judged another person. What was the outcome?

## CONTEMPLATE

Make a list of the sins in your life that you'd like to conquer. Outline your path to living a life without these sins by identifying specific steps you're willing to take to live a life that is pleasing to God.

# RULES VS. RELATIONSHIPS

*"If you are convinced that you are a guide for the blind, a light for those who are in the dark, an instructor of the foolish, a teacher of little children, because you have in the law the embodiment of knowledge and truth— you, then, who teach others, do you not teach yourself? You who preach against stealing, do you steal? You who say that people should not commit adultery, do you commit adultery? You who abhor idols, do you rob temples? You who boast in the law, do you dishonor God by breaking the law?" (Romans 2:19-23 NIV)*

---

**W**hat if the people who you care most about came to their conclusions about God and all of Christianity by simply observing your life? That's a lot of pressure, isn't it? The truth is that many adults who have no relationship with God or his church became discouraged and disillusioned early in their lives after witnessing the inconsistent behaviors of those who called themselves Christians. When our words don't match our actions, there's much more at risk than someone simply calling us a hypocrite. Paul didn't miss the opportunity to admonish the self-righteous Jews and privileged Gentiles who preached one set of rules but followed another.

No matter where you are in your personal journey, it's often a good idea to stop and hit the proverbial "reset" button and acknowledge this one important fact: we are all guilty before God and fall short of his glory. We don't measure up. When we take an inward look and focus on our own shortcomings and sinful behaviors, we are much less likely to spend our time assessing the sinfulness of others. Paul used this opportunity to tell the Jewish members of the Roman Church that they should teach themselves the law before attempting to teach others. There's something very valuable in that message for each of us.

Jesus is actually the first person in history to talk about "hypocrisy." He took the concept from the Greek word for actor: hypocrite. Hypocrites wore masks on stage to denote their role. Thus, hypocrisy is playacting. It's acting like you're something you're not. A hypocrite (like a Pharisees) acted like he was perfect, when, in fact, his life was a moral disaster. So a Christian fights hypocrisy not merely by bringing his life into alignment with his words, but also by being transparent about his sin. A Christian should always be candid: I am not perfect. I make mistakes. I am often a mess. My words are often out of alignment with my actions.

## MY PRAYER

*God, soften my heart so that I can begin to build relationships built on trust and understanding rather than rules. Give me the courage to open my life to others so that they can see the pain and struggle in my life. Let them also see the great reward I've been given by my choice to give my life to you. I pray for these things in the name of your son, Jesus Christ. Amen.*

## READ: MATTHEW 7:1-6

**QUESTION #1:** What are the wounds in your life that you'd be willing to share with another man to help him better understand the journey that lies before him?

**QUESTION #2:** What are the parts of your life that are inconsistent with the Christian life you'd like to lead?

## CONTEMPLATE

Write a prayer to God asking him to increase his presence in your life to help you address the sinful behavior that prevents you from being completely transparent in the presence of others.

# THE CLEAN SLATE

*This righteousness is given through faith in Jesus Christ to all who believe. There is no difference between Jew and Gentile, for all have sinned and fall short of the glory of God, and all are justified freely by his grace through the redemption that came by Christ Jesus. (Romans 3:22-24 NIV)*

My earliest memories in life are that of my experiences while attending a parochial school, where much of my education was strongly influenced by religion. Somewhere along the way, I developed a very twisted perspective that God was constantly watching over me with his heavenly scorecard, keeping a record of every sin. Before I was old enough to understand the concept of confessing my sins, I worked diligently to try and balance out good deeds with the sins I couldn't seem to avoid as a child. For every piece of penny candy I inadvertently slipped into my pocket at the local drugstore, I made sure that I atoned for this sin by offering to sweep off my neighbor's front porch or picking up a piece of litter along the street. Because I seemed to always come up short on good deeds, I began to view God as the deliverer of punishment. I feared God, indeed, but in all the wrong ways.

Throughout most of my life, I had heard that Jesus paid the price for my sins on the cross; however, it wasn't until I was 45 years old that I began to understand what it was like to have a personal relationship with Jesus Christ. It was then that I discovered that my sins were forgiven by God. Jesus took the penalty for my sin and gave me his righteousness in return. This means that God, the perfect judge, no longer declares a "guilty" verdict over my life, but instead "innocent." This is what Paul calls "justification." And it's the best news a guilty person like me could ever hear. All we have to do is believe that Christ died for our sins, ask for forgiveness of our sins and then receive Christ into our lives.

In the Graeco-Roman world, when a benefactor gave a gift, they expected the gift to produce certain results. Thus, a good gift accomplished the giver's intended effect. A poor gift failed. God freely gives us the gift of salvation without qualification. But he is an extraordinary gift giver, which means that his gift should have an effect on your life: becoming more like his son. We are called to live lives that honor God and that respect the tremendous sacrifice paid by Jesus on that cross. We must move forward understanding that God hates all sin, no matter how minor the infraction may seem. Being angry is the same as committing murder. Being lustful is the same as committing adultery. Our relationship with God is not transactional, it's transformational.

## MY PRAYER
*God, thank you for your gift of salvation and for justifying me through faith in spite of my unworthiness. Help me to avoid sin and to stand strong against all that is evil in this world. I ask for your forgiveness of my sins as I boldly proclaim you as my savior and redeemer. I pray for these things in the name of your son, Jesus Christ. Amen.*

### READ: JOHN 1:5-10

**QUESTION #1:** Do you believe that your sins can be forgiven by simply asking Jesus into your life and asking for forgiveness?

**QUESTION #2:** What changes do you need to make in your life that will enable you to avoid sin?

### CONTEMPLATE

Just as Jesus has forgiven us of our sins, we, too, should extend forgiveness to those who have sinned against us. Write a note to someone who needs to receive your forgiveness.

# NO ROOM FOR DOUBT

*Yet he did not waver through unbelief regarding the promise of God, but was strengthened in his faith and gave glory to God, being fully persuaded that God had power to do what he had promised. This is why "it was credited to him as righteousness." (Romans 4:20-22)*

---

I f you've ever prayed for a miracle or asked God to deliver on a special request, you may have found yourself feeling a sense of doubt when things didn't go as you hoped. The story of Abraham and Sarah (Genesis 17-23) is a wonderful account of what happens when we remove doubt or hesitance from our relationship with God. As the story goes, the Lord appeared before Abraham and told him that he would have a son and that his offspring, if they were obedient to God, would be given the land of Israel. Abraham was more than 100 years old and Sarah was 90. While Sarah chuckled at the thought of having a son, Abraham took God at his word and never doubted that God's promise would hold true. Most of us can relate to Sarah's skeptical nature. After all, she was unable to have children. At this late stage in life, it did not seem possible that she could become pregnant.

There's so much to learn from Abraham's unstoppable faith. As the story progresses, 25 years pass between God's promise and the birth of Sarah and Abraham's son, Isaac. When you put these details in the context of our own relationships with God and the absurd nature of our expectations, you can't help but feel ashamed by the shallow depth of your faith. The lesson here is that we need to trust God, even when the odds seem completely impossible. If God makes a promise, the depth of our faith is inconsequential. God's word is absolute. When Abraham shifted his focus from his circumstances and inadequacies, his faith grew stronger and he intently believed that God would come through. God's promises always come to fruition through human trust.

In Isaiah 41:10 we hear the words, "So do not fear, for I am with you; do not be dismayed, for I am your God. I will strengthen you and help you; I will uphold you with my righteous right hand." The Jews in Rome needed to be reminded that God had honored his covenant with Abraham. The same is true for each of us. Like Abraham, we must keep our focus on God and not the troubles in our lives. God should be the source of our courage and confidence to keep moving forward. There's no room for doubt in our relationship with God.

## MY PRAYER

*God, give me the faith of Abraham and the forbearance to know that you are always with me, protecting me and strengthening me. Let me shift my focus from my troubles to deepening my relationship with you. I pray for these things in the name of your son, Jesus Christ. Amen.*

## READ: 1PETER 5:1-7

**QUESTION #1:** Recall a time in your life when your faith wavered. What were the circumstances?

**QUESTION #2:** Think of a person in your life who you completely trust. What are the obstacles that prevent you from putting that same kind of trust in God?

## CONTEMPLATE

The Greek word for "faith" can also be translated as "allegiance." This makes sense, because trusting God always entails giving him your allegiance. Write a pledge of allegiance to God, and then pray through it.

*"For the wages of sin is death, but the gift of God is eternal life in Christ Jesus our Lord."*

**(Romans 6:23 NIV)**

# WEEK 2

# PUSHING THROUGH

*Therefore, since we have been justified through faith, we have peace with God through our Lord Jesus Christ, through whom we have gained access by faith into this grace in which we now stand. And we boast in the hope of the glory of God. Not only so, but we also glory in our sufferings, because we know that suffering produces perseverance; perseverance, character; and character, hope. And hope does not put us to shame, because God's love has been poured out into our hearts through the Holy Spirit, who has been given to us. (Romans 5:1-5 NIV)*

When you read about the life of the Apostle Paul, you learn a lot about the trials he faced while working to grow the early Christian church. When he wrote this letter to the Roman church, he was in prison, one of the many times he would be held in captivity. During his ministry, he was beaten with rods, whipped, stoned, and exposed to long periods of hunger. In spite of all of this, he took his suffering in stride, finding joy through the pain knowing that he was serving God's kingdom. Each of us will face tough times over the course of our lives. Perhaps it's a cancer diagnosis, the loss of a loved one, or fighting through addiction. These trials have nothing to do with God testing us or punishing us for our past sins. God, however, does use these moments to shape and mature us with the hope of making us into the image of Christ.

In James 1:2-4, we are reminded that our suffering produces endurance. Through these moments of endurance, we become more spiritually mature, growing in confidence and hope. These trials deepen our reliance on God while building our character and giving us a permanent standing in God's grace. James tells us to find joy in these moments because of how they affect us. When we compare our suffering to that of Paul's, we realize that things could be much worse. When we view our trials in their proper perspective, we begin to understand that God is indeed pulling us through our troubles and developing us into better citizens of his kingdom.

When all is said and done, you will see that God is on your side and that he has always been there with you every step along the way. He is our provider, protector, comforter, and redeemer. Knowing this should give us a greater sense of confidence about the future. The things we once feared are no longer obstacles. The once impossible aspirations are now within reach. The hurts and pains we've experienced have contributed to our character. The trials we faced have made us stronger and better and closer to God. The next time a challenge comes your way, embrace it, knowing that it is yet another opportunity to grow in Christ.

### MY PRAYER
*God, give me the confidence to overcome the trials in my life. Help me to recognize my challenges as opportunities that will help me grow closer to you. For these things, I pray in the name of your son, Jesus Christ. Amen.*

### READ: JAMES 1:2-8

**QUESTION #1:** What would you say has been the biggest trial in your life?

**QUESTION #2:** In what way did you grow or mature as a result of that trial?

### CONTEMPLATE

Create a timeline of your life starting with the year you were born up to the present day. Take a moment to mark the happiest moments in your life. Note the sad or troubling times as well. How have these milestones shaped you into the person you are today?

# SACRIFICIAL LOVE

*But God demonstrates his own love for us in this: While we were still sinners, Christ died for us. Since we have now been justified by his blood, how much more shall we be saved from God's wrath through him! (Romans 5:8-9 NIV)*

What is the meaning of love these days? You can love your mother, but you can also love a new restaurant. You can love your neighbor but you can also love a photo someone shares on social media. We've become somewhat carefree in the way we throw around the "L" word. Perhaps you've heard that there are four distinct types of love described in the ancient Greek language. Storge is the love that a parent feels for a child. Phileo is used to describe the idea of brotherly love. Philadelphia is the city of brotherly love. And, of course, there's eros love that describes the emotions felt in a sexual relationship. This is where we get our English word, "erotic." Agape love describes the kind of love that is sacrificial in nature. God demonstrated sacrificial love for us when he sent his son to die for our sins on the cross. More than simply laying down one's life for another, sacrificial love is in a dimension all unto its own.

Most of us view love in very different ways. Too often, the love we share with others is transactional or reciprocal. We love people because they love us. We love people because they are part of our family. We love people because they are simply fun to be around. Sometimes, to make a point or to punish someone, we withhold our love as if it were an allowance or stipend that must be earned. To put things in the proper perspective, it's important to remember that we didn't "earn" God's love. His love for us came with no restrictions or conditions. His love is everlasting….past, present, and future. Can you make that same absolute claim about the love you feel for another person? What if they betray or hurt you in the worst imaginable way? Would you still love them?

In John 15:13, we hear the words, "Greater love has no one than this: to lay down one's life for one's friends." While this seems like the ultimate sacrifice, it still pales in comparison to the love given to us by God. He loved us while we were his enemies. No further sacrifice or deed is required on our part. God loved us as his own, long before any of us ever turned to him. As men of Christ, we should model Christ's example by striving to deny ourselves and sacrificially loving others with no expectation of anything in return.

## MY PRAYER

*God, make my heart capable of feeling sacrificial love for others. Teach me to place a renewed importance of sharing agape love, no matter the circumstances. Let me live more like Christ with every passing day. I pray for these things in the name of your son, Jesus Christ. Amen.*

## READ: 1 CORINTHIANS 13:1-13

**QUESTION #1:** In spite of your perceived unworthiness, are you capable of accepting God's sacrifical love? Why or why not?

**QUESTION #2:** Outside of spiritual pursuits, why do you find it difficult to accept things you haven't earned?

## CONTEMPLATE

Write a prayer thanking God for his sacrificial love. Include ways that you can accept this gift and pay it forward to the people in your life.

# THE TWO ADAMS

*Consequently, just as one trespass resulted in condemnation for all people, so also one righteous act resulted in justification and life for all people. For just as through the disobedience of the one man the many were made sinners, so also through the obedience of the one man the many will be made righteous. (Romans 5:18-19 NIV)*

You can probably remember a time as a child when you were specifically warned by an adult not to do something. Maybe you were told to stay away from a creek or not to cross a busy street. In spite of the strict warnings you received, you couldn't resist the urge to tempt fate and disobey the rules. Even as an adult, you probably still struggle with temptation and the urge to do something that you know you're not supposed to be doing. That was Adam's problem in the Garden of Eden. Adam gave in to the temptation that Satan had craftily used to lure him in. Unfortunately, Adam's disobedience turned out to be a death sentence for all the generations to follow and the seed that would become man's predisposition to sin.

Adam functioned as God's representative for all humanity—past and present. His failure is our failure. His disobedience to God introduced death and sin to the world. It's important to understand that there is a difference between being a sinner and leading a sinful life. But Adam is not the only representative of humanity. Jesus is a second representative. Which means that his righteousness can be our righteousness. All humans must choose who they want to represent them: Adam or Jesus? If you choose Jesus, his death gives you a clean slate with God. Adam's act of disobedience was wiped clean by Jesus' righteous act of self-sacrificial love. God allowed Jesus to die for our sins. His righteousness and sacrifice on our behalf canceled out the fate that Adam had secured on our behalf.

You can't just say a prayer, and then move on with life. You need to live a life of continual repentance. In John 1:12 we learn, "Yet to all who did receive him, to those who believed in his name, he gave the right to become children of God." By believing in the death and resurrection of Christ and accepting him as your savior, your death sentence can be commuted and God will welcome you into eternal life. Despite this knowledge, many of us will slide back into our rebellion and disobedience to God. As men, we have an innate propensity toward the kind of sin that can turn our lives upside down, ruin relationships, and drive us into isolation. When we come to our senses, in deep remorse for our indiscretions, we still have a God who loves us. Like the prodigal son, we will be welcomed home.

## MY PRAYER

*God, give me the power to resist sin and temptation. Make me obedient in all aspects of my life. Help me to feel worthy of the sacrifice that Christ exchanged for my sin. I pray for these things in the name of your son, Jesus Christ. Amen.*

## READ: 1 CORINTHIANS 15:20-28

**QUESTION #1:** Do you believe that you are capable of living a life that is increasingly free of sin?

**QUESTION #2:** What measures can you take to reduce the presence of sin in your life?

## CONTEMPLATE

Spend a moment thanking God for sending Jesus to counter the disobedience of Adam and the forgiveness of our sins.

# UNDESERVED GRACE

*Do not offer any part of yourself to sin as an instrument of wickedness, but rather offer yourselves to God as those who have been brought from death to life; and offer every part of yourself to him as an instrument of righteousness. For sin shall no longer be your master, because you are not under the law, but under grace. (Romans 6:13-14 NIV)*

P erhaps at some point in your life, you've been welcomed into a prestigious organization that is held in high esteem by your peers and by others in the community. Perhaps it was an honor society in high school, a branch of the military, or a noteworthy service organization. As part of the initiation process, it is made clear to you that there are expectations in terms of your conduct and how you manage your affairs. Your actions now reflect on every member of the entire organization as their actions reflect on you. You have been called to uphold a standard. Shouldn't this also be true in our relationship with God? Once we've accepted the gift of God's salvation, we should be willing to set aside our sinful ways, standing firm against all sin, but especially our desires related to lust, greed, and envy.

Sin can be a vigorous and destructive force in our lives. Unfortunately, sin will always be in our lives regardless of how hard we work to avoid it. But once we become members of God's family there is an expectation that we must no longer allow sin to control us. We have to decide whether we are going to give in to the weaknesses of our flesh or if we're going to serve God. There's no doubt that each of us will stumble along the way and prove ourselves to be unworthy. Here's the good news: God will never withdraw his grace from us, no matter how badly we fail. That's pretty amazing when you consider that we did nothing to earn God's grace. This amazing gift is part of God's unique nature and not the result of any attempt on our part to earn favor through good deeds and clean living.

In Titus 2:12, Paul lays out his instructions for the bishops and elders of the church telling them to "say no to ungodliness and worldly passions, and to live self-controlled, upright and godly lives." The same is expected of us. We are no longer slaves to the sin of Adam but rather slaves to the righteousness of a loving God who has extended an unimaginable grace. Paul literally opens Romans by calling himself a "slave of Christ Jesus." Unfortunately, our translations render it as "servant." While no repayment is demanded, we would be wise to choose God over sin at all times and heed his call to do good and serve others. Now that we're members of God's prestigious family, it's time we started acting like it.

### MY PRAYER

*God, thank you for your gift of grace. Give me the wisdom and self-control to honor the trust you placed in this most generous act. Give me the strength to overcome sin and set my eyes on serving you the remaining days of my life. I pray for these things in the name of your son, Jesus Christ. Amen.*

### READ: TITUS 2:1–15

**QUESTION #1:** Which type of sin in your life is the most difficult to set aside?

**QUESTION #2:** What are some of the ways that you can honor God's grace through service to others?

### CONTEMPLATE

Write a confession of your sin to God, asking for forgiveness and the discipline to move toward a life free from sin.

# A NEW LIFE

*But thanks be to God that, though you used to be slaves to sin, you have come to obey from your heart the pattern of teaching that has now claimed your allegiance. You have been set free from sin and have become slaves to righteousness. (Romans 6:17-18 NIV)*

I f you've ever known anyone who has been the recipient of an organ transplant, you probably know that the first emotion they experience is joy. When they first get the news, they feel as if they've been given a second chance or a new lease on life. There will, of course, be feelings of fear and trepidation before the surgery, but those emotions seem pale in comparison to that overall feeling of exuberance and hope for a new future. In a like manner, Paul reminds us that when we join God's family, we, too, get a new life. When it happens, sin has lost its power over us and we begin to feel the transformation taking place from within. We should still be deeply mindful of the consequences of sin we've experienced but we can now rejoice because we know we've been liberated.

Gone is the emptiness, depression, and despair that was once part of our sinful past. Our new lives promise a sense of joy, peace, and contentment that we haven't experienced in a very long time. But with the blessings of this new life comes a responsibility to live obediently in God's word. If someone gives you their heart so you can live, you dishonor the gift if you pollute it with nicotine and cholesterol. The teachings in the Bible are clear communication from God on how we should live our new lives. We are no longer slaves to our sinfulness, but rather slaves to the righteousness of God. Like a child who spent years in an orphanage, our adoption into God's family gives us the company of the Holy Spirit and the gift of eternal life in heaven. Once adopted, we must be willing to let our lives be used for God's purpose. We should cast aside evil and focus our energies on doing good and serving others.

Even with this adoption, we are still free agents, perfectly capable of choosing which master we want to serve. You can't serve two masters. It's impossible to live a life that pleases God and Satan. In John 3:36, we are told, "Whoever believes in the Son has eternal life, but whoever rejects the Son will not see life, for God's wrath remains on them." It's your choice. Whichever you choose, remember that people don't end up in hell because they led sinful lives. People end up in hell because they've rejected Christ. Those who repent and accept Christ as their savior will find the joy and peace that comes with being adopted into God's family.

## MY PRAYER

*God, thank you for releasing the stranglehold that sin once had on my life. Let me embrace the adoption into your family and make clear that I have chosen to follow you, not by my words, but by my actions. I pray for these things in the name of your son, Jesus Christ. Amen.*

## READ: EPHESIANS 1:3-14

**QUESTION #1:** We often treat sin like an old friend or seductress. How would your life change if you saw sin as a slave master?

**QUESTION #2:** Does the promise of salvation seem too good to be true? Does your unbelief hold you back?

## CONTEMPLATE

Take a moment to thank God for the gift of salvation. Ask for forgiveness of your sins and seek his guidance on how you might better serve his purpose.

*You, however, are not in the realm of the flesh but are in the realm of the Spirit, if indeed the Spirit of God lives in you. And if anyone does not have the Spirit of Christ, they do not belong to Christ.*

**(Romans 8:9 NIV)**

# WEEK 3

# A SLAVE TO SIN

*We know that the law is spiritual; but I am unspiritual, sold as a slave to sin. I do not understand what I do. For what I want to do I do not do, but what I hate I do. And if I do what I do not want to do, I agree that the law is good. As it is, it is no longer I myself who do it, but it is sin living in me. For I know that good itself does not dwell in me, that is, in my sinful nature. For I have the desire to do what is good, but I cannot carry it out. For I do not do the good I want to do, but the evil I do not want to do— this I keep on doing. Now if I do what I do not want to do, it is no longer I who do it, but it is sin living in me that does it. (Romans 7:14-20)*

W hen I decided to recommit my life to Christ as an adult, I felt pretty confident that once baptized, I would come out of that water as a new man. There I stood soaking wet before my family, friends, and the entire congregation of my church. I was anxious to get out of my wet clothes and get started with my new life. On my way home from church that evening, a reckless driver cut me off in traffic and nearly caused an accident. I laid on my car horn and yelled some very "un-Christian" words at the guy. It dawned on me that my baptism had not, in fact, made me perfect. I still had plenty of work to do in terms of actually living out a Christian life. Knowing the rules of Christian living is not enough. I discovered that all of the self-determination in the world wasn't going to make me a better man, let alone righteous.

It took a while for me to discover that being a Christian is a lifelong process. As much as I wanted to be "that guy," I was going to have to struggle to get even close to what I had envisioned for myself being a good Christian man. Nearly 15 years after committing my life to Christ, I still find myself taking a few steps forward, and inevitably, a couple

of steps back. There's no doubt that I'm making progress but I would
have never imagined the twists, turns, bumps, curves, and potholes that
would attempt to derail my Christian journey. Admittedly, most of my
struggles have been self-inflicted. There's no magic pill you can take that
makes the temptation toward sin go away. When I'm not deeply rooted,
I still feel the gravitational pull of lust, greed, gluttony, and selfishness.

In 2 Corinthians 12:9-10, we are reminded that God's grace is sufficient
and made perfect when we experience our weakest moments. In times
like these, we must lean into God's grace and pray that the Holy Spirit
will give us the power to navigate through our weakness, giving us the
strength to resist Satan's claim over our hearts. We have to make the
conscious decision whether we're going to be tempted by sin or owned
by sin. The choice is ours.

### MY PRAYER
*God, help me embrace the process required to become a follower of Christ.*
*Give me the fortitude to turn from sin and pursue you with all my heart.*
*When I am weak, you are strong. I pray for these things in the name of*
*your son, Jesus Christ. Amen.*

### READ: 2 CORINTHIANS 12:1-10

**QUESTION #1:** Which type of sin is most likely to derail your Christian
journey?

**QUESTION #2:** What steps can you take to protect yourself from the
temptation to sin?

### CONTEMPLATE

Write about your Christian journey. What surprised you most about the
process? Describe the distractions and detours that slowed the process.
Are you satisfied with where you are now?

# TUG OF WAR

*Now if I do what I do not want to do, it is no longer I who do it, but it is sin living in me that does it. So I find this law at work: Although I want to do good, evil is right there with me. For in my inner being I delight in God's law; but I see another law at work in me, waging war against the law of my mind and making me a prisoner of the law of sin at work within me. What a wretched man I am! Who will rescue me from this body that is subject to death? Thanks be to God, who delivers me through Jesus Christ our Lord! So then, I myself in my mind am a slave to God's law, but in my sinful nature a slave to the law of sin. (Romans 7:20-25)*

Y ou've probably had occasion to play a game of "tug of war" at some point in your life. The point of the game is to determine which team has the strength to pull the opposing team across a centerline. Depending on how well-matched the teams are, you will typically see one team get pulled a few feet closer to the line, and then the energy shifts and the other team gets pulled toward the center. In the most interesting matchups, you'll see a lot of moving back and forth... and a whole lot of heaving and groaning. In many ways, our spiritual journeys are very much like this game. The closer we move to God, the harder the devil tries to pull us back toward sin. Like the tension in the rope, we feel that same sensation of being pulled in the wrong direction.

In our daily walk, we face the frequent struggle between knowing what is right and doing what is right. The path of least resistance is simply giving in to the desires of our flesh and choosing sin over righteousness. Satan is trying to win the battle for our hearts and minds and most of us are ill-equipped to effectively fight back. We lack a battle plan. Paul reminds us that spending time in God's word strengthens and gives us an understanding of the principles we should be living out in our daily lives. There is power in knowledge and we can equip ourselves by spending time in the word. We can protect ourselves if we put on the full armor of God that relies on righteousness, truth, faithfulness, and the readiness that comes from knowing God's word.

You are not alone in this battle. If Paul struggled with sin, you can be assured that every other man you know is facing this same conflict between good and evil. Even men who do honorable works on the outside are still grappling with sin on the inside. As much as we want to be delivered from sin, we won't be completely free until we meet Christ in eternity. If a perfect sin-free life is not attainable on this earth, we should redirect our energies to living the best Christian life we can. Do your best to win the battles you can while leaning into the Holy Spirit and by saying "yes" more often to God and "no" to the things that tempt you. You will be given the strength you need for even the toughest challenges you encounter.

## MY PRAYER

*God, give me the strength I need to win the war against Satan. Protect my heart and mind from evil and help me equip myself with the truth and readiness that comes from knowing your word. For these things, I pray in the name of your son, Jesus Christ. Amen.*

### READ: EPHESIANS 6:10-20

**QUESTION #1:** Describe a time your fight with sin felt like a real battle.

**QUESTION #2:** Recall a time in your life when you felt you were being pulled toward sin.

### CONTEMPLATE

Make a list of the steps you can take to better equip yourself against the power of sin. How will you incorporate these steps into your daily life?

# GREAT EXPECTATIONS

*Therefore, brothers and sisters, we have an obligation—but it is not to the flesh, to live according to it. For if you live according to the flesh, you will die; but if by the Spirit you put to death the misdeeds of the body, you will live. For those who are led by the Spirit of God are the children of God. (Romans 8:12-14)*

I f it feels good, do it! That's the motto that a lot of men have embraced at different points in their lives. Whether it was driven by adolescent hormones, newfound independence after going off to college, or a renewed sense of freedom following a divorce, some of us have developed a prolific skill for living in the moment. Because of that, we all know guys who really struggle to resist these same temptations when they decide to put their lives back on the right track. Paul makes it pretty clear that we can't have it both ways. Each of us has to choose whether or not we're going to pay homage to the desires of the flesh or pursue the Holy Spirit with all our hearts.

When we are adopted into God's family, we accept an increased level of responsibility for our actions and the personal choices we make. A lot of guys had their dads say something like this, "Son, you are a Parry. Parrys work hard. Parrys are respectful. Parrys take responsibility. When you're lazy, disrespectful, and irresponsible, your actions give our family a bad name. I love you, so I hope you'll make our family proud." That's probably an unfair amount of pressure to put on a kid. My dad told me what to do, but he wasn't very patient when I failed. He didn't always come alongside me to encourage me and empower me. God is a good father. His spirit is a guide. Perhaps we should look at these as the

"Christian family's values." If you're going to take the name of Jesus, this is what it looks like to live up to the family name.

The best way to overcome the power of sin in your life is to tap into the power of the Holy Spirit, which gives us the remarkable ability to stand up to the temptations that drag us down. The great news is that the Holy Spirit will guide us through our recovery. The Holy Spirit will reveal to us a new sense of truth in our lives and help us to gain a new understanding of God's word. Best of all, the spirit will direct us to other believers who will be anxious to help us in our spiritual development. In Galatians 5:22, Paul tells us that the fruits of the spirit are "love, joy, peace, forbearance, kindness, goodness, faithfulness, gentleness and self-control."

## MY PRAYER
*God, help me to appreciate both the privilege and the responsibility of becoming a member of your family. Guide me to the Holy Spirit that I, too, will have conquering power over the sin in my life. For these things, I pray in the name of your son, Jesus Christ. Amen.*

### READ: GALATIANS 5:13-26

**QUESTION #1:** Describe a time that God's spirit was trying to guide you, but you resisted and went the other way?

**QUESTION #2:** What can you do in your daily routine to more frequently tap into the Holy Spirit?

### CONTEMPLATE

Write about the fruits of the Holy Spirit that you desire to have most in your life. Explain why.

# AN ETERNAL PERSPECTIVE

*I consider that our present sufferings are not worth comparing with the glory that will be revealed in us. (Romans 8:18 NIV)*

If you've read through the Book of Acts, you probably have a pretty good idea of the suffering that the Apostle Paul endured as he traveled, proclaiming the message and the teachings of Jesus. He was imprisoned on multiple occasions, flogged, stoned, and publicly humiliated. He was shipwrecked for three months. Given the circumstances of his mission, you can imagine that he also dealt with periods of hunger, exhaustion, and mental anguish. Oddly enough, Paul never complained about his circumstances. He had an eternal perspective that kept his focus on the glories that awaited him after his resurrection. While most of us have never been flogged or shipwrecked, we do face the challenges that come with a cancer diagnosis, natural disasters, and moments of sudden loss and tragedy. Paul encourages us to look at our troubles with a fresh perspective by staying focused on our eternal rewards as followers of Jesus.

Paul wants us to endure through our suffering with a sense of hope. The glories that will be revealed to us in heaven far outweigh any pain that might come from the temporary suffering experienced on this earth. The majestic nature of resurrected life will be infinitely more satisfying and meaningful than we could ever begin to imagine. The splendor we will experience is a remarkable gift given only to God's adopted heirs. To prepare for eternal life, we must adopt a spirit of godliness in our earthly lives and make decisions based on how they affect our eternal life rather than the here and now.

When Warren Buffet was a nobody, and Berkshire-Hathaway was just a dream, he was looking for new clients. He asked his next-door neighbor how much money he had socked away for his daughter's college expenses. Warren told his neighbor to invest it with him, but the neighbor refused. It turned out to be a $450,000,000 mistake. If the neighbor had a crystal ball, he would've invested everything with Buffet, but he couldn't see into the future. So he didn't. In a like manner, Christians do know the future, and God is offering us something far better than $450,000,000. So why do we get fixated on this life, rather than investing in what really counts?

## MY PRAYER

*God, grant me the discipline to keep my focus always on the eternal perspective. Let me ponder, day and night, the wondrous glories of eternal life as a member of your adopted family. Let these thoughts change the way I make decisions and live my life on this earth. I pray for these things in the name of your son, Jesus Christ. Amen.*

### READ: 2 CORINTHIANS 4:7-18

**QUESTION #1:** Looking back over your life, what have been your most intense moments of suffering?

**QUESTION #2:** Would having an eternal perspective change the way you approach the work you do?

### CONTEMPLATE

Write about the most challenging period you've experienced in your life. Now, apply an eternal perspective to the context of this time in your life. How does this affect your perspective on that time? Is there any joy or purpose that can be found from that period of suffering?

# EARNEST EXPECTATIONS

*"For the creation waits in eager expectation for the children of God to be revealed. For the creation was subjected to frustration, not by its own choice, but by the will of the one who subjected it, in hope that the creation itself will be liberated from its bondage to decay and brought into the freedom and glory of the children of God." (Romans 8:19-21)*

Have you ever waited for something in such eager anticipation that it completely dominated your every thought? Perhaps it was the arrival of Christmas morning when you were a child or maybe a very special vacation for which you had scrimped and saved every dime and nickel for a long period of time. Maybe it's your daughter's wedding day or the arrival of a new car you ordered six months ago. Too often, when those highly anticipated moments come and go, there's often this anticlimactic range of emotions that leave you feeling sad and disappointed that the moment passed so quickly. Paul uses his letter to the Roman church to remind us that God has something very special planned for his followers that will be so unimaginably wonderful that it should be captivating our minds, minimizing every other care or concern we might have. Paul assures us that when the moment arrives, there will be nothing anticlimactic about it.

Paul is speaking of the renewal of creation when Christ returns to reveal a renewed heaven and earth. At the same time, the curse of man's sinfulness will be reversed and death, pain, and suffering will be abolished forever. Man's capacity for sin will be eliminated and the world of sin and death, as we know it now, will be eliminated. In Revelation 21:1-8, we learn that this renewed creation will be experienced by those who believe and have placed their faith in Jesus and the sacrifice he made for us on the cross. As we watch this world decay and society move into a further state of disarray, we are reminded to keep a watchful eye fixed on the promise that God will renew all things (Acts 3:21).

Until that time arrives, we are called to go into the world with Christ fighting evil, healing the sick, feeding the hungry, and ministering to widows and orphans. In the midst of this work, we can find strength and sustenance in knowing that the Second Coming of Christ is in our future. The curse on this world that came because of Adam's sin is nearly gone and, with one fell swoop, all that is evil will disappear into the ether. Those who rejected Jesus and refused to believe will be sentenced to a second death in the fiery lake of sulfur. As believers, we will be resurrected into renewed bodies, freed from our desire to sin. Our adoption into God's family will be complete and we will be welcomed into the world we were always meant to live in, a place far better than we could ever imagine.

## MY PRAYER

*Father, God, grant me the wisdom and fortitude to more eagerly anticipate the renewed creation you have planned. Help me to shift my priorities and focus so that I can more completely prepare for the return of Jesus by serving others and teaching them about this triumphant day when we experience a renewed heaven and new earth. I pray for these things in the name of your son, Jesus Christ. Amen.*

## READ: REVELATIONS 21

**QUESTION #1:** How would having an eager anticipation of the renewed creation change the manner in which you live out your daily life?

**QUESTION #2:** What steps can you take now to assure that your loved ones will be with you in the renewed creation?

## CONTEMPLATE

Make a list of the things that currently cause you pain and suffering that will vanish in the new creation.

*What, then, shall we say in response to these things? If God is for us, who can be against us? He who did not spare his own Son, but gave him up for us all— how will he not also, along with him, graciously give us all things?*

**(Romans 8:31-32 NIV)**

# WEEK 4

# IN GOOD TIMES AND BAD

*And he who searches our hearts knows the mind of the Spirit, because the Spirit intercedes for God's people in accordance with the will of God. And we know that in all things God works for the good of those who love him, who have been called according to his purpose. (Romans 8:27-28 NIV)*

I f you've ever made a cake from scratch, you know that it requires a diverse combination of ingredients. If you were to taste the individual ingredients you would discover that some are sweet, but others are bitter and rather undesirable. It's hard to conceive that the combination of these elements would create something so delicious and wonderful. The same is true for the experiences we encounter in our lives. There are moments of exuberance and there are times of deep sorrow. There are good times and, of course, there are challenging times. Everyone experiences the highs and lows of life. In the end, when our time on this earth is over, most of us will look back and say, "You know, I've had a pretty good life."

We can take comfort in knowing that God has his hand in every event in our lives. It's difficult for most people to understand that a God who loves as he does, could possibly allow the death of a child or for cancer to take the life of an amazingly good person. Like the ingredients of a cake, God, in his infinite wisdom, combines the good and bad moments in our lives for our ultimate good. The sum total of these experiences has been directed and masterfully orchestrated by a God who loves us, unconditionally. While God is in full control, He still gives man the free will to make choices, even those he does not agree with. God does not predetermine evil. When a man commits an evil act against another man, God notices and deals with the evil in a manner he sees fit.

You may recall the story of Job and the extent of his suffering. Through all of it, he stayed faithful to God. In Job 1:21, his words resonate, "The Lord gave, and the Lord has taken away. Blessed be the name of the Lord." The stronger our faith and the deeper our knowledge is of God's true nature, the more we learn to not resent the pain in our lives. God is present and with us through all of this and his ultimate goal is to make each of us more like Christ. All of this requires trust and patience and a deep confidence that God is working for the good of those who love him.

## MY PRAYER

*God, teach me to be thankful for all of the events in my life, both good and bad. Give me the faith and patience of Job as I navigate the twists and turns, always believing that your plan is a good and perfect plan. I pray for this in the name of your son, Jesus Christ. Amen.*

## READ: 1 JOHN 3:1–3

**QUESTION #1:** How has God turned a hardship in your life into something good?

**QUESTION #2:** What did God want to teach you through that hardship, and how did God change you through it?

## CONTEMPLATE

Make a list of the major events in your life where you suspect God may have played a key role. List the highs and lows. What are the moments that now seem God-ordained?

# GOD'S GOT YOUR BACK

*"What, then, shall we say in response to these things? If God is for us, who can be against us? He who did not spare his own Son, but gave him up for us all—how will he not also, along with him, graciously give us all things?" (Romans 8:31-32)*

O ne of the things we discover as we become husbands and fathers is the profound impact our parents and other influential figures have had on how we process our emotions. For instance, if you went through a season of life as an adolescent where you made some bad choices (and got caught), there's an excellent chance that you probably disappointed your parents at some point along the way. If you screwed up in school or made a mistake on the football field, you probably also disappointed a teacher or coach. If you've damaged the family's reputation or embarrassed someone you greatly respect, you might have experienced what might have seemed like the withholding of love. Unfortunately, bad parenting skills can sometimes be hereditary and passed on from one generation to the next. While, of course, parents are always going to love their children, sometimes the only way we know to send a clear message is to stop expressing the love we feel for a child who has caused us pain.

One of the speed bumps I encountered in my spiritual journey was trying to wrap my head around the differences between my earthly father and my heavenly father. I believed, right or wrong, that my biological father was often disappointed in the choices I made as a young adult. Over time, I had the strong sense that he had inadvertently decided to withhold his love from me. When I began to pursue a relationship with God, I was dumbfounded by his unconditional love for me. The notion was almost inconceivable, but I know now that it was real. God has demonstrated his immense love for me on countless occasions. Perhaps the most reassuring and comforting aspect of being a Christian is knowing that God's got my back, even when I make bad choices. "If God is for us, who can be against us?"

The comfort and confidence that come from knowing God's incomparable love are transformative in so many ways. Once again, it's a gift I didn't earn. However, I can take comfort in knowing that God's grace and mercy will pull me through the darkest and most challenging moments of my life. In 1 John 4:16, we find these words of wisdom, "And so we know and rely on the love God has for us. God is love. Whoever lives in love lives in God, and God in them." God will never withhold his love for you. We would all do well to follow his example and break the generational curse of withholding love from the important people in our lives.

## MY PRAYER

*God, thank you for your gift of unconditional love. Let me show that same type of love for others and, in doing so, teach others about Your ways. Give me the wisdom and strength to know when I am withholding love. I pray for these things in the name of your son, Jesus Christ. Amen.*

## READ: DEUTERONOMY 7:7-15

**QUESTION #1:** How are you withholding your love from someone who is close to you?

**QUESTION #2:** How has your relationship with your earthly father shaped your perception of your heavenly father? How are they similar and different?

## CONTEMPLATE

Recall a time in your life when felt as if someone's love was being withheld from you. What were the circumstances? What is the current status of your relationship with that person?

# BLESSED ASSURANCE

*For I am convinced that neither death nor life, neither angels nor demons, neither the present nor the future, nor any powers, neither height nor depth, nor anything else in all creation, will be able to separate us from the love of God that is in Christ Jesus our Lord. (Romans 8:38-39 NIV)*

I f you've raised children, you might remember the delicate balancing act you had to walk in trying to make them aware of the dangers that exist in the world around them without making them fearful of society as a whole. When I was young, the messages included not taking candy from strangers and looking both ways before crossing the street. Today, making your children aware of looming dangers is a more difficult task. Thanks to technology, our children have to be warned about predators on the internet and gaming systems. Unfortunately, we also have to talk to kids about what to do when another kid brings a gun to school. We want our kids to savor the innocence of youth, but we also want them to be on guard against a myriad of dangers. God wants to offer us that same kind of protection. He wants us to have an acute awareness that evil exists and that Satan is always preying upon our vulnerabilities.

Our sinfulness can manifest itself in many forms. In Mark 7:21-22, we are told, "For it is from within, out of a person's heart, that evil thoughts come—sexual immorality, theft, murder, adultery, greed, malice, deceit, lewdness, envy, slander, arrogance and folly." Satan knows which of these sins is most likely to lure us away from Christ. Once we take a bite of that apple, he traps us and uses our sinfulness against us. He's not stopping there. The Evil One will use his powers to make you feel helpless and then attempt to pull you away from Christ. As men, we become easy targets for Satan when we find ourselves in isolation, either at home, on a business trip, or cut off from other men who will hold us accountable.

Satan gained victory with Adam in the Garden of Eden but fell in defeat when Christ died for our sins on the cross at Calvary. Thus, nothing can separate us from God. We may face sickness, injury, or other peril, but God will never abandon us. God wants us to be confident and convicted in the reality that we are eternally secure with him. God may not take away our problems, but he will always take us through our problems. You can be assured of that very important promise.

## MY PRAYER

*God, I cling to your promise that you will protect me from the evil in this world. Help me to live a life that honors your promise. Give me the strength I need to defeat Satan. I pray for these things in the name of your son, Jesus Christ. Amen.*

## READ: JAMES 1:2-18

**QUESTION #1:** How do you plan to guard yourself the next time you are tempted by sin?

**QUESTION #2:** Do you feel isolated? Can you think of another man or group of men who would be willing to help keep you from sin?

## CONTEMPLATE

Describe your feelings in knowing that God will protect you from evil. Identify the sin or the circumstances where you feel most vulnerable and susceptible to being separated from God.

# HUMILITY

*But who are you, a human being, to talk back to God? Shall what is formed say to the one who formed it, "Why did you make me like this?" Does not the potter have the right to make out of the same lump of clay some pottery for special purposes and some for common use? (Romans 9:21 NIV)*

H ave you ever played a board game or cards with someone who suddenly changes the rules in the middle of the game? Everything seems to be progressing along just fine and, out of nowhere, this person pulls the rug out from under you. That's probably how the Jewish people felt when they discovered that following the law of Moses and doing good deeds did not make them righteous in God's eyes. To make matters worse, when they found out that Gentiles had a path to salvation even while ignoring the law, they cried "foul!" You can be assured that God didn't change the rules for salvation, the Jewish people just misunderstood them. From Abraham to Moses to David, God always rescued humans by grace, not on the basis of their moral merit. Becoming a member of God's family never required a perfectly moral resume. It only required trust.

Being declared righteous before God comes only through a professed faith in Christ. Given their disbelief that Jesus was the Messiah certainly complicated things for some Jews. Despite their claims of living by the law, Paul knew they were on shaky ground because no man is capable of completely following the law. The Israelites had a very difficult time admitting their failure to do so. They believed they could "earn" salvation. The path to righteousness is found only through Jesus Christ. Jesus was the only hope for bridging the gap between man and God.

Like the Jews, our pride is usually what stands between us and God. As men, we operate under a foolish premise that we can somehow be self-sufficient and do things all on our own. We are blinded by the myth of self-reliance. Our stubbornness and insistence that we do things our own way can drive a wedge between us and God. As hard as we may try, we're never going to change God's rules. We can go to church every week, volunteer to serve widows and orphans, contribute our entire wealth to those less fortunate, but we're never going to be right with God until we humble ourselves and accept Jesus Christ as our savior.

## MY PRAYER

*God, thank you for blessing my life in the way that you have deemed appropriate. Keep me humble and guide me to a place where I can silence my pride and arrogance. I know that I have received many blessings thatI don't deserve. May I always approach you with an unstoppable spirit of gratitude. For these things, I pray in the name of your Son, Jesus Christ. Amen.*

## READ: JEREMIAH 18:1–10

**QUESTION #1:** When do you feel most self-reliant in life?

**QUESTION #2:** When do you feel most weak, unprepared, and needy?

## CONTEMPLATE

Make a list of the God-given talents you have been blessed with. Have you given credit where credit is due? Make a plan for sharing your gratitude for these gifts.

# THE KEY TO SALVATION

*Brothers and sisters, my heart's desire and prayer to God for the Israelites is that they may be saved. For I can testify about them that they are zealous for God, but their zeal is not based on knowledge. Since they did not know the righteousness of God and sought to establish their own, they did not submit to God's righteousness. Christ is the culmination of the law so that there may be righteousness for everyone who believes. (Romans 10:1-4 NIV)*

---

As men, we tend to look for shortcuts that will save us time and get us there faster. Some of us will drive in the HOV lane to get us to work faster even though we're by ourselves in the car. Sometimes we'll call in a favor with a buddy who's connected to score tickets to a sporting event rather than waiting in line like all the other schmucks. Some of us will even turn a T-shirt inside out and spray it with a squirt of cologne to avoid having to do a whole load of laundry. If we can save time, save money, or save a little hassle, we don't think twice about cutting corners. When it comes to our spiritual journeys, there are no corners to cut. If we want to have a relationship with God, we have to go through Jesus.

Paul admonished the Israelites because while most believed in God, many did not believe in Jesus Christ. As the passage above reads, they were zealous for God, but they were missing the most important piece of the puzzle. In John 14:6, Jesus made it pretty clear by saying, "I am the way and the truth and the life. No one comes to the Father except through me." The relationship between God and man was broken in the Garden of Eden, but God promised to one day send a Messiah to restore that relationship. God became man in the form of Jesus Christ and by dying on the cross, our sins were taken away and our relationship was restored. For those who choose not to embrace this important aspect of theology, there is no path to God.

Some people believe that there are many paths to God, but Paul would not concur. Whereas all other religions give you a set of good deeds to accomplish to get up the mountain, Christianity is the only faith that tells the story of God coming down. This is why Jesus is the only way. Left to your own devices, you will never climb the mountain. And thanks to him, you don't have to.

## MY PRAYER

*God, thank you for the gift of salvation and the opportunity to anticipate an eternal life in your presence. Let me live a life that is worthy of this most holy covenant with mankind. For these things, we pray in the name of your son, Jesus Christ. Amen.*

### READ: JOHN 14:5-14

**QUESTION #1:** In what aspects of your spiritual life have you cut corners or made shortcuts?

**QUESTION #2:** What are the ways you try to earn God's favor apart from Jesus?

### CONTEMPLATE

Write about your motivation to continue doing good works even after understanding that these deeds have little to do with earning the gift of salvation.

*Therefore, I urge you, brothers and sisters, in view of God's mercy, to offer your bodies as a living sacrifice, holy and pleasing to God—this is your true and proper worship.*

**(Romans 12:1 NIV)**

# WEEK 5

# TWO STEPS AWAY

*If you declare with your mouth, "Jesus is Lord," and believe in your heart that God raised him from the dead, you will be saved. For it is with your heart that you believe and are justified, and it is with your mouth that you profess your faith and are saved. (Romans 10:9-10 NIV)*

One of the many reasons people give for not reading the Bible regularly is that they find it confusing and sometimes hard to understand. There are a lot of names of people and places of which they've never heard and the effort required to understand the historical context of events can be overwhelming. Unfortunately, there are many reasons why Biblical literacy is decreasing in our society and, as a result, fewer people can understand the breadth and depth of God's true nature. Romans 10:9-10, however, is as clear and straightforward of a message that you can find in the Bible. And thankfully, the simple proposition found in these two verses is the key to salvation.

If you believe in your heart that Christ was risen from the dead and you then confess with your mouth that Jesus is Lord, God welcomes you into eternal salvation. Sounds pretty simple, right? All you have to do is believe in your heart and confess with your mouth. Well, it wasn't such an easy proposition for many of the Jews to whom Paul was teaching. The people of Israel rejected God because they did not believe that Jesus was the true Messiah. Therefore, because they could not accept this one important truth, they could not be saved.

It is said that what the heart believes, the mouth confesses. In Paul's time, expressing one's faith in Christ was proof of genuine salvation.

Publicly confessing one's faith in Christ often led to persecution and severe punishment, and even execution. In anticipation of the consequences, one would have to have a deep conviction that they had been saved and would be protected by God. Today, the risks associated with professing our belief, trust, and confidence in Christ are minuscule. It's still a simple proposition and the reward is as magnificent as it was in the days when Paul walked the earth.

## MY PRAYER

*God, thank you for the gift of salvation. Give me the courage to profess my faith in Christ in all that I do. Guide me so that I can deliver the keys to salvation to those who do not know you. Let my actions speak louder than my words. I pray for these things in the name of your son, Jesus Christ. Amen.*

## READ: DEUTERONOMY 30:11-14

**QUESTION #1:** What obstacles keep you from confessing your sin and submitting your life to Jesus?

**QUESTION #2:** How is God calling you to recommit your life to Jesus, or to accept him as your king today?

## CONTEMPLATE

Make a list of the people in your life who need to hear about God's promise of salvation. What steps can you take with each person to help them believe and then confess their faith in Christ?

# TOO GOOD TO THROW AWAY

*"I ask then: Did God reject his people? By no means! I am an Israelite myself, a descendant of Abraham, from the tribe of Benjamin. God did not reject his people, whom he foreknew. Don't you know what scripture says in the passage about Elijah—how he appealed to God against Israel: "Lord, they have killed your prophets and torn down your altars; I am the only one left, and they are trying to kill me?" And what was God's answer to him? "I have reserved for myself seven thousand who have not bowed the knee to Baal." So too, at the present time there is a remnant chosen by grace. And if by grace, then it cannot be based on works; if it were, grace would no longer be grace. What then? What the people of Israel sought so earnestly they did not obtain. The elect among them did, but the others were hardened." (Romans 11:1-7 NIV)*

---

If you're like me, you probably have a basement, garage, or storage area filled with leftover scraps of wood, carpeting, or tile that were simply "too good to throw away." If we can be honest with one another, we set aside these remnants with the most sincere hope that one day, they will become an integral part of another project or be of great value to another person. "Just in case," we say to ourselves as the stack grows taller and wider. In his letter to the Romans, we can see that Paul shared a similar attitude about the small number of Jews who chose to believe in God's promise of salvation and he referred to them as the "faithful remnant." While small in number, these followers were powerful and passionate in their faith, and most importantly, they trusted God. When you lack strength in numbers, passion can make a big difference.

Perhaps it's because we have the benefit of witnessing God's goodness over these last 2,000 years, but one thing we know for sure is that God always makes good on his promises. But still, there were many who rejected God's truth. Today, there are still some who refuse to accept this good news despite the overwhelming body of proof. Our pride causes us to reject these gifts because we feel they call into question our sense of self-sufficiency.

Jesus spoke to his followers in parables because he knew that many would be unable to accept the truth that others found so easily. When there is no spiritual hunger or effort put forth to understand, it's a lost cause and a missed opportunity. In a world where it's sometimes hard to recognize the strong presence of Christians around us, it's understandable how some might doubt the realness of God. As a result, many men have hardened hearts and have become incapable of hearing or seeing God's work throughout the universe. Paul teaches us that when we become cut off from God, there's rarely a "second chance" for gaining God's favor. At some point, we reject God so thoroughly that he gives us entirely over to our sin. We don't know when. We only know that every tiny of act of resistance is another step closer to losing the war. It is utter foolishness to wait for the "right time" to follow Jesus. That time will never come, and the moment will always be too late.

## MY PRAYER

*God, soften my heart so that I might comprehend your greatness. Help me to receive your gift of grace and abundant mercy. I pray for these things in the name of your son, Jesus Christ. Amen.*

## READ: ISAIAH 29:10-16

**QUESTION #1:** How are you resisting God and hardening your heart to his will?

**QUESTION #2:** Who in your life is hardening himself to God? How is God calling you to lovingly, graciously confront him?

## CONTEMPLATE

Write a prayer of Thanksgiving acknowledging the promises of God.

# RENEWING OUR MINDS

*Do not conform to the pattern of this world, but be transformed by the renewing of your mind. Then you will be able to test and approve what God's will is—his good, pleasing, and perfect will. (Romans 12:2 NIV)*

'I've noticed that when I'm around a group of guys, I behave very differently than I do when I'm alone with my wife. I've also noticed when I'm in a professional setting, I take on yet another personality and set of behaviors. I find myself conforming to the situation and circumstances depending on whom I'm with. Looking back, I suppose it's always been that way. From a very young age in elementary school to when we're playing checkers in the nursing home, we have this uncanny desire to fit in, to be liked, to be included. Sometimes being part of the crowd requires you to say and do things you wouldn't do if your pastor were sitting next to you. Paul reminds us that setting our standard for behavior on the cultural norms of this world is foolish. The world is like a flock of starlings, cutting left and right, up and down, without any rhyme or reason. You can try and fit in, but you will end up going nowhere.

Like the ugly caterpillar transitioning into a beautiful butterfly, God wants us to transform from our superficial lives and find the path that's not traveled by the rest of the world. God wants us to march to the beat of a different drummer. God wants us to meet life's challenges by thinking Biblically about our relationships and our role on this earth. He's not asking us to abandon culture and go live in a cave. He's asking us to be more diligent in discerning the difference between good and bad when we make choices. It won't be easy, but nothing worthwhile ever is.

The first step in this process simply involves surrendering ourselves to the will of God and putting our complete trust in Christ. In Jeremiah 29:11, we are reminded that the Lord has "plans to prosper you and not to harm you, plans to give you hope and a future." The second step is to set boundaries for ourselves. We know the circumstances that are typically at play when we make bad decisions. Whether we're isolated, angry, intoxicated, or around women we are not married to, we are vulnerable to sin. We must avoid the triggers that cause us to slide down the slippery slope that was our old lives. It's at times like this that we need to put on the breastplate of righteousness described in Ephesians 6:14 and protect ourselves against Satan who wants to see us fail. Renewing our minds with the confidence that God always wins is a step in the right direction.

### MY PRAYER

*God, help me to recognize your good, pleasing and perfect will. Lead me through a transformation so that I can lose my old life and exchange it for an eternal life with you. I pray for these things in the name of your son, Jesus Christ. Amen.*

### READ: EPHESIANS 6:10-18

**QUESTION #1:** Under what circumstances do you notice a change in your behavior?

**QUESTION #2:** Recall a time in your life when you didn't fit in with the crowd. How did you modify your behavior under those circumstances?

### CONTEMPLATE

Write about the things in your life that you want to change in your walk with God. What steps are you willing to take to begin that process?

# OUR TRUE SELF WORTH

*For by the grace given me I say to every one of you: Do not think of
yourself more highly than you ought, but rather think of yourself with sober
judgment, in accordance with the faith God has distributed to each of you.
For just as each of us has one body with many members, and these members
do not all have the same function, so in Christ we, though many, form one
body, and each member belongs to all the others. (Romans 12:3-5 NIV)*

W e all have those moments when we find ourselves feeling deeply
remorseful for something we've done. In the aftermath of our
mistake, we try to process our emotions hoping desperately
to find what it was that triggered our behavior. More often than not,
if we're being honest with ourselves, there is usually some feeling of
insecurity tied to our childhood or dysfunction from our family of
origin. To make matters worse, we attempt to justify our failure by
comparing our behaviors to that of another guy who has fallen short
in a way that makes our stupidity look like a moment of brilliance. We
say to ourselves, "Well, at least I didn't cheat on my wife like Bob did."
Setting our moral compass by worldly standards usually means that
we're setting the bar way too low.

In Galatians 6:1-6, we are instructed to test our actions without
comparison to others. This is especially important when you understand
that living your life by earthly standards will most often cause us to
overestimate our own righteousness. Just because you're better than Bob
doesn't mean you measure up to the expectations that God has for you.
Granted, life may be more comfortable when the bar is set low; however,
in the end, you still must face the judgment of God.

Our self-worth should be inextricably woven into the relationship we have with Christ. Apart from this relationship, we really have nothing of our own that we can brag about. Our righteousness is relative, but God's righteousness is real. We must celebrate the fact that we have been given his grace and compassion in spite of our many shortcomings. And yet, we should feel motivated to raise the bar and live our lives in a way that honors God. In the end, the measure of a good life won't be a balance sheet or scorecard, but rather by the way we lived our lives in accordance with the example set for us by Jesus Christ.

## MY PRAYER

*God, grant me the wisdom to live my life in pursuit of the righteousness you have modeled so well. Give me the discipline to raise my bar to a standard that honors you. I pray for these things in the name of your son, Jesus Christ. Amen.*

### READ: GALATIANS 6:1-6

**QUESTION #1:** What aspects of your life fall short of the standard you set for yourself?

**QUESTION #2:** Identify an area of your life where you have set the bar low, based on worldly standards.

### CONTEMPLATE

Write about someone you know who lives their life by a high standard. What part of their behavior could you emulate in your life?

# ALL IN FOR CHRIST

*Love must be sincere. Hate what is evil; cling to what is good. Be devoted to one another in love. Honor one another above yourselves. Never be lacking in zeal, but keep your spiritual fervor, serving the Lord. Be joyful in hope, patient in affliction, faithful in prayer. Share with the Lord's people who are in need. Practice hospitality. (Romans 12:9-13 NIV)*

---

All of us have probably provided instructions or directions to someone only to discover later that they didn't fully comprehend what it was you were asking them to do. The next time you give instructions to that person, out of an abundance of caution, you go out of your way to give instructions in a very clear and concise manner. You are succinct and direct, leaving nothing for misinterpretation. Some might say that Paul wanted to make it very clear what was expected of new Christians as they pursued living their lives in a manner that would please God. Paul's rapid exhortation of these 13 commands leaves little room for misunderstanding. Now that these new followers had embraced the tenets of Christianity, it was time to make their behavior match those beliefs.

Most of Romans 12 lays out instructions for Christian living once a person's heart and mind have been transformed and renewed. Chief among the priorities was to develop a fierce rejection of all that was evil. Many Christians today can recognize sin; however, they just seem incapable or unwilling to hate it as they should. Truth be told, many of us are simply going through the motions making half-hearted attempts to live a Christian life. It's as if we want to put one foot planted in the hope that comes with our new life, but still keep one foot in our old life where we were more tolerant of our own sin. God doesn't want to use our faith to hide our sins. He wants to use it to kill them.

Throughout our lives, many of us have been conditioned to pretend to love others. Often guided by societal standards that dictate that we be kind and polite, this superficial kind of "love" is too often rooted in ulterior motives or our own hypocrisy. Paul calls on us to lean into our renewed minds and find an enthusiastic joy in serving and loving others. He wants us to be "all in" when it comes to living the Christian life. He wants to have a zeal for helping others and to maintain a high level of energy, enthusiasm, and diligence in our generosity toward others. At the end of each day, we should look forward to asking ourselves, "How can I better serve my brother tomorrow?" By embracing these principles, we will grow by honoring one another and sharing genuine love with our fellow Christians.

## MY PRAYER

*God, teach me to hate all that is evil and embrace all that is good. Give me an unbridled enthusiasm for serving others and extending genuine love to those in my life. I pray for these things in the name of your son, Jesus Christ. Amen.*

## READ: 1 CORINTHIANS 12:12-31

**QUESTION #1:** What are the obstacles that prevent you from enthusiastically serving others?

**QUESTION #2:** Who is God calling you to serve enthusiastically today?

## CONTEMPLATE

Make a list of 10 things you could do, starting tomorrow, to serve others.

*Do not take revenge, my dear friends, but leave room for God's wrath, for it is written: "It is mine to avenge; I will repay," says the Lord.*

**(Romans 12:19 NIV)**

# WEEK 6

# THE ART OF FORGIVENESS

*Do not repay anyone evil for evil. Be careful to do what is right in the eyes of everyone. If it is possible, as far as it depends on you, live at peace with everyone. Do not take revenge, my dear friends, but leave room for God's wrath, for it is written: "It is mine to avenge; I will repay," says the Lord. On the contrary: "If your enemy is hungry, feed him; if he is thirsty, give him something to drink. In doing this, you will heap burning coals on his head." Do not be overcome by evil, but overcome evil with good. (Romans 12:17-21)*

Jesus often taught his most valuable lessons by sharing parables. This form of storytelling was effective because it made important principles easier to understand, especially when it came to difficult or awkward subjects. In Matthew 18:21-35, Jesus tells the Parable of the Unforgiving Servant. You may recall the story of the master having pity and forgiving the debt owed to him by one of his servants. When the master finds out that this same servant did not extend forgiveness of a much smaller debt, he was outraged, demanded full payment, and then imprisoned the unmerciful servant when he was unable to pay. The parable reminds us that God, the master of the universe, has forgiven us the debt of our sins... past, present, and future. He wants us to pay forward his grace and mercy by forgiving those who we believed have sinned against us.

Men know how to hold grudges. Many of us still remember the kid on the grade school playground who bullied us when we were in the second grade or the guy who cut us off in traffic a couple of weeks ago. Forgiveness is much more than pardoning someone for his or her misdeeds. It's about seeking reconciliation and making an attempt to extend kindness to someone we consider an enemy. When we choose to seek revenge or retaliate against someone who has wronged us, we only escalate a bad situation. God calls on us to take the high road in these situations. We should be the first to extend an olive branch and make amends.

I think about all the times on Twitter that someone posts something nasty about someone else… but then the "someone else" replies and shows kindness in return. Maybe they apologize for a misdeed or an unkind word. The entire situation is defused. This is the ultimate defense of God's reality. We don't have to know six arguments for the existence of God. The bar is so much lower. We just need to be kind. That's it. Be kind. People will be so shocked, they might convert on the spot.

## MY PRAYER
*God, humble my heart so that I will have the humility to forgive those who have sinned against me. Teach me to love my enemies as much as I love my family. Give me the wisdom to remember that only you can deliver justice. I pray for these things in the name of your son, Jesus Christ. Amen.*

## READ: MATTHEW 18:21-35

**QUESTION #1:** What is the name of one person to whom you should extend forgiveness?

**QUESTION #2:** What is the name of a person from whom you should seek forgiveness?

## CONTEMPLATE

Write about a grudge against someone that you have carried with you for a long period of time. What steps can you take today to extend peace and grace to that person?

# RESPECT AUTHORITY

*For the one in authority is God's servant for your good. But if you do wrong, be afraid, for rulers do not bear the sword for no reason. They are God's servants, agents of wrath to bring punishment on the wrongdoer. (Romans 13:4 NIV)*

Those who claim that religion and politics don't mix may not be aware of the connection between God and our governmental authorities. Paul tells us that those who have been elected or appointed to positions of authority are actually servants of God, put in place to provide order in our society, protect the good, and punish those who break the law. Because justice and peace are integral parts of our society, God's hand is in the process of choosing those who will carry out his will. As long as we are doing good and contributing to that sense of order, we have nothing to fear from government leaders who are fair and just.

Through elections and appointments, God uses the collective will of the people to create a system of organized justice. There are limitations, of course, as to how much power and authority these leaders are given. There will also be times when the will of government does not align with the will of God. For example, when a government allows the destruction of innocent life or leniency to a person who has taken another's life, we're duty-bound to challenge officials in a respectful, but stern, manner. We must remember that Paul lived in a radically different context than us. The Roman Empire was an oppressive regime that ruled by violence and severe taxation. Christians had virtually no power to effect change in the government. So we must imagine what Paul might say to us—those who live in a representative democracy. Would he not say that our responsibility is even greater because we do have a voice, and the ability to change our governing authorities?

Jesus taught us that God's kingdom is not of this world. When the Herodians and the Pharisees attempted to trick Jesus on the issue of paying taxes, Jesus pointed to the picture of Caesar on the coin and said, "give back to Caesar what is Caesar's, and to God what is God's." Of course, Caesar wanted the wealth and power that comes from collecting taxes, but what he ultimately wanted was the allegiance and loyalty that people feel for the one absolute God. There will be leaders like Caesar, Mussolini, and Adolph Hitler who rule with evil and hatred, but those examples are the exception rather than the rule. A peaceful and organized government that operates by Biblical principles punishes evildoers, and provides for the poor is what God has in mind. We should pray for our leaders and be respectful of the role they play in our society.

## MY PRAYER
*God, I pray for the leaders in our local, state, and federal governments. Give them the blessings of wisdom, discernment, empathy, and a heartfelt desire to serve others. Protect them and guide them through these divisive times. I pray for these things in the name of your son, Jesus Christ. Amen.*

## READ: 1 PETER 2:13-17

**QUESTION #1:** How does knowing that our government leaders are chosen servants of God affect your view of politicians?

**QUESTION #2:** In what ways have you witnessed a government act in a way that is inconsistent with Biblical principles?

## CONTEMPLATE

Make a list of the ways that your local government could do a better job of serving the less fortunate living in your community. What steps can you take to bring these needs to the attention of elected officials?

# LIVING IN THE LIGHT

*The night is nearly over; the day is almost here. So let us put aside the deeds of darkness and put on the armor of light. Let us behave decently, as in the daytime, not in carousing and drunkenness, not in sexual immorality and debauchery, not in dissension and jealousy. Rather, clothe yourselves with the Lord Jesus Christ, and do not think about how to gratify the desires of the flesh. (Romans 13:12-14)*

The plot of the 1998 movie, *The Truman Show*, featured Jim Carrey in the role of Truman Burbank, who, unknown to him, was the star of a reality TV show about his life. Every move that Truman made was captured by an elaborate arrangement of cameras hidden from view. In some ways, this movie conjures up images of George Orwell's book, *1984*, where Orwell predicts a Totalitarian society with mass surveillance systems watching all of us. A modern-day version of this scary plot is the reality TV show, *Big Brother*, where a dozen souls all choose to live in a house that has cameras in every room watching their every move. Imagine yourself living in a world where everything you said and did was displayed for the whole world to see. Would those circumstances cause you to modify your behavior or the choices you make daily? Of course, it would.

In his letter to Romans, Paul uses the example of daylight and darkness to illustrate our transition from the sin of our secret lives to living in the light in anticipation of the return of Christ. If we believed that the return of Christ was going to take place in the immediate future, would we change the way we live? Paul encourages us to live in the light so that sin cannot take hold in our lives. If you have a friend with whom you have established a trusting relationship, you will see that giving your sin the "light of day" by sharing it can be a very liberating experience. The sin we work so hard to hide from other people becomes manageable when we expose it and come to terms with the power it holds over us. One could argue that we already live in this world. Everything we do online is tracked and processed by artificial intelligence. Machine learning uses that data to predict your future behavior and sell it to advertisers. What if your wife, or your boss, or your kids could see everything those machines see?

The best way to avoid sin is to avoid the circumstances and conditions that feed into our struggle with temptation. For some of us, it's consuming too much alcohol. For others, it may be a desire to slip into isolation. When we're at home alone or on a business trip, the temptation to view pornography may overcome us. The best way to avoid sin is to expect and anticipate the return of Christ. Knowing that your sins are not hidden from God should motivate you to live a more honorable life.

### MY PRAYER
*God, give me the discipline to live a life that can be exposed for all to see. Give me the strength to resist temptation and the circumstances that expose my weakness. I pray for these things in the name of your son, Jesus Christ. Amen.*

### READ: EPHESIANS 4:17-22

**QUESTION #1:** Which of your sinful behaviors would you least like being exposed to people who know you?

**QUESTION #2:** What person in your life could be your most trusted accountability partner?

### CONTEMPLATE

Create a timeline that captures the events, activities, and interactions from the last 24 hours of your life. What are the things on that list that you'd feel ashamed about if exposed for all to see?

# BREAKING DOWN THE FACADE

*So then, each of us will give an account of ourselves to God. Therefore let us stop passing judgment on one another. Instead, make up your mind not to put any stumbling block or obstacle in the way of a brother or sister. (Romans 14:12-13)*

The influence of social media has exacerbated a problem that man has struggled with for decades. Amid our insecurities and our feelings of inadequacy, many of us create a facade to shield the rest of the world from seeing what our lives are really like. The pictures we post on social media platforms tend to only reflect the most attractive and interesting parts of our lives. Whether it's a family photo, vacation pics, or an elegant meal you've recently enjoyed in an upscale restaurant, we project an image that our lives are near perfect. This kind of activity puts an awful strain on our circle of friends. They know that their life doesn't measure up to the glamour that is supposedly the norm in our lives. In the verses above, Paul is using this opportunity to call out the Christians who, in a like manner, are creating a facade about their religious convictions and their moral superiority over new converts. Jews used their food laws and sabbath regulations to suggest that they were spiritually superior to Gentiles. The Gentiles returned the favor, laughing at the Jews for all their rules and bragging about their freedom. Yet, even if these acts fooled their fellow humans, they never fooled God.

Of course, God knows what our lives are really like. He knows our darkest secrets and our most shameful sins. In Hebrews 4:13, we are told that "nothing is hidden from his sight. All things are naked and open to the eyes of God, to whom we must give account." On the one hand, God has removed our sin from us. On the other hand, he's deadly serious about it.

Our conversations with God on judgment day will not be about our sins but rather how we used our time, treasures, and talent to serve others.

Paul also reminds us that it's not our place to judge others. That responsibility lies alone with God through the power he gave his son. We will be measured by how we encouraged the weak and helped new Christians advance in their personal journeys. Being legalistic and judgmental with others does more harm than good in advancing God's kingdom. Ultimately, these actions cause new believers to stumble and turn away from God. We are all accountable to Christ and we should not think higher of ourselves than we do of others. In the end, when you stand before God on judgment day, He won't be interested in talking about the sins of others. His focus will be entirely on you.

## MY PRAYER

*God, teach me to be an encourager of young Christians and lead me to a place where I have no desire to judge others. Let me live a life that is consistent so that I can tear down the facade of shame and be revealed as a dedicated follower of Christ. I pray for these things in the name of your son, Jesus Christ. Amen.*

### READ: HEBREWS 4:12-13

**QUESTION #1:** How do you portray your life on social media or to people outside your immediate circle of friends?

**QUESTION #2:** How can you encourage new believers to grow into mature and dedicated followers of Christ?

### CONTEMPLATE

Make a list of new Christians who would benefit from your encouragement with regard to their journeys. In what specific ways can you help them to mature in Christ?

# FINDING COMMON GROUND

*May the God who gives endurance and encouragement give you the same attitude of mind toward each other that Christ Jesus had, so that with one mind and one voice you may glorify the God and Father of our Lord Jesus Christ. Accept one another, then, just as Christ accepted you, in order to bring praise to God. (Romans 15:5-7 NIV)*

We live in divisive times. It seems that everywhere you turn, you see some person or some group drawing a line in the sand and refusing to compromise on even the simplest or most esoteric of issues. Whether it's politics, religion, or how to respond to a pandemic, there seems to be little room for compromise. We've forgotten how to meet those with differing viewpoints in the middle. While it's always been okay to disagree with others, we seem to approach every tiny disagreement with outrage and disdain. The Roman church was made up of diverse people with different ethnicities and religious backgrounds and Paul uses this opportunity to call his readers to common ground.

The word "tolerance" seems to be a popular buzzword these days. Current cultural influences suggest that we try to do a better job of simply tolerating people who are different than us. Paul wants us to take it one step further and actually love those who are not like us. What does that look like? First, you have to stop and acknowledge those you encounter and let them know that you see them. Second, you have to be willing to intently listen to their stories and understand where they're coming from and the situational factors that have affected them in their journeys. For most of us, this is a major step outside of our comfort zones. We've become accustomed to passing people on the sidewalk without making eye contact or extending the courtesy of a nod, let alone a full-blown acknowledgment.

In John 13:34, Jesus commands his disciples to "Love one another. As I have loved you, so you must love one another." What does that look like more than 2,000 years later? In this era of social media and text messages that have pushed us away from face-to-face communication, it means we need to roll the clock back and do some old-fashioned communicating. It means we need to invite people who are different from us into our homes to break bread and let down our defenses. It's about eliminating racial and economic discrimination from our lives. It's about actively seeking out people who may scare us just a bit and extending a smidgeon of the grace that God has extended to us. We must find ways to begin accepting others in the same manner in which Christ accepted us.

## MY PRAYER

*God, soften my heart so that I can begin to accept others as Jesus Christ accepted me. Give me the courage to be the first to extend the hand of friendship and reconciliation. Let me do all of this with a contrite heart and an authentic spirit. I pray for these things in the name of your son, Jesus Christ. Amen.*

## READ: JOHN 13:34-35

**QUESTION #1:** Is there a person or group of people with whom you can initiate building an unexpected, but extraordinary relationship?

**QUESTION #2:** What steps can you take to break out of your comfort zone and build a relational bridge with someone who is homeless, imprisoned, or economically challenged?

## CONTEMPLATE

Write about the personal comforts you are willing to risk to reach out to someone who is totally unlike you. What are the barriers that might keep you from enthusiastically pursuing this?

# ADDITIONAL RESOURCES

**FredParry.Life**

**Becoming The Man God Intended You To Be**

Interested in using this book for a small group or Bible study?
Visit our website for FREE study materials, discussion questions,
handouts, rules of engagement for small group participants,
and other teaching tools.

Looking for a speaker for your next men's event?

Contact Fred Parry,
711 West Broadway, Columbia, Missouri 65203
or email fparry61@gmail.com